SPORTS SUPERSTARS

AARON RODGERS

By Kevin Frederickson

Kaleidoscope
Minneapolis, MN

Your Front Row Seat to the Games

This edition is co-published by agreement between Kaleidoscope and World Book, Inc.

Kaleidoscope Publishing, Inc.
6012 Blue Circle Drive
Minnetonka, MN 55343 U.S.A.

World Book, Inc.
180 North LaSalle St., Suite 900
Chicago IL 60601 U.S.A.

Kaleidoscope ISBNs
978-1-64519-035-6 (library bound)
978-1-64494-191-1 (paperback)
978-1-64519-135-3 (ebook)

World Book ISBN
978-0-7166-4337-1 (library bound)

Library of Congress Control Number
2019940054

Printed in the United States of America.

TABLE OF CONTENTS

CHAPTER 1

A Super Finish

Aaron Rodgers stands at the 12-yard line. His right leg is shaking. He looks nervous. The quarterback has three seconds to hike the ball. If not, it's a **penalty**. Rodgers yells out to his teammates. It is the fourth quarter of the biggest game in American sports. His Green Bay Packers are in Super Bowl XLV.

The Packers **snap** the ball in time. Rodgers looks to the left. He sees nothing but Pittsburgh Steelers. Rodgers looks to his right. He sets his feet. He looks down the field. Wide receiver Greg Jennings breaks free.

FUN FACT
Rodgers beat the rival Chicago Bears to go to the Super Bowl.

Aaron Rodgers looks to throw in Super Bowl XLV.

Where Rodgers Has Been

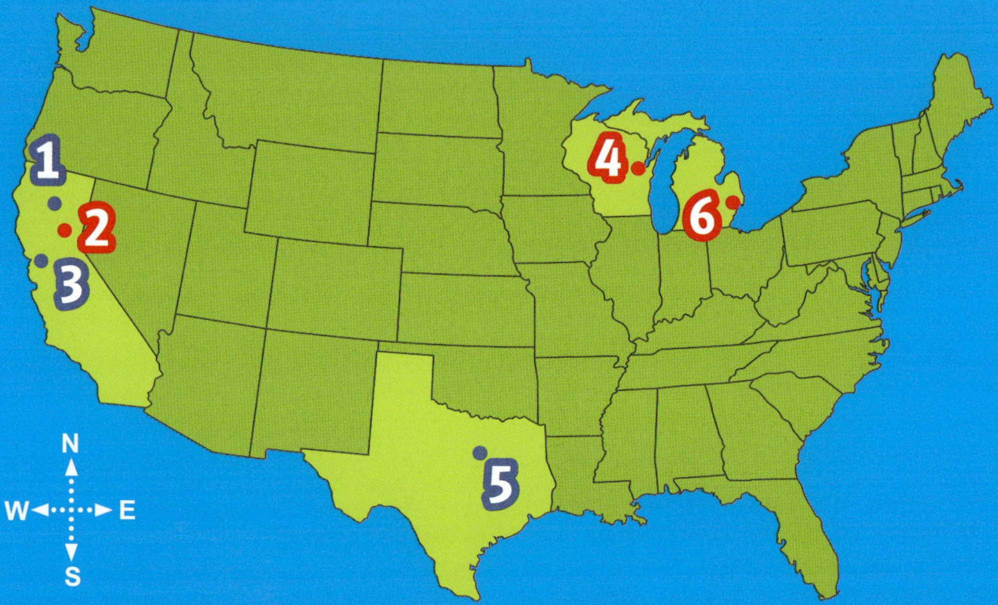

1. **Chico, California:** Rodgers was born here.
2. **Oroville, California:** Rodgers played here for Butte Community College.
3. **Berkeley, California:** Rodgers played two seasons here at the University of California.
4. **Green Bay, Wisconsin:** Rodgers plays here with the Green Bay Packers.
5. **Arlington, Texas:** Rodgers won Super Bowl XLV with the Packers here after the 2010 season.
6. **Detroit, Michigan:** Rodgers completed his first successful Hail Mary against the Detroit Lions here inside Ford Field.

Rodgers moves his arm back. He lifts his back foot and lets go of the ball. It is a bullet of a throw. Jennings is there. He waits in the corner of the end zone. He jumps up and grabs the ball. He quickly puts both of his feet down. The referee puts his arms in the air. Touchdown!

The fans in the stands roar. Rodgers runs to a teammate. They hug. The Packers lead the Steelers 28–17. There are still 11 minutes left in the game.

The Steelers come back to score. But it is not enough. Green Bay runs out the clock to win.

Rodgers celebrates a touchdown with teammate Jordy Nelson.

The players dance and celebrate. Workers place a large stage on the field. Rodgers takes his place on the stage. He **grins** from ear to ear. He lifts up a large trophy. At the top is a silver football. It is the Lombardi Trophy. It goes to the team that wins the Super Bowl. Rodgers raises it high above his head. Confetti lands on him. His hat and shirt have the same words on them. They say, "Super Bowl Champions."

Rodgers was just 27. But he was already one of the greatest quarterbacks to ever play in the National Football League (NFL).

CHAMPIONSHIP BELT

Rodgers runs toward the end zone. He looks to avoid defenders. Rodgers tiptoes his way in to score. Touchdown! He spikes the ball. He has a smile on his face. Rodgers puts his hands together at his waist. Then he quickly moves them apart. He pretends to wear a championship wrestling belt. That became his famous touchdown celebration. After winning the Super Bowl, Rodgers put on a real championship belt.

Rodgers holds up the Lombardi Trophy after winning Super Bowl XLV.

CHAPTER 2

Working His Way Up

Aaron Rodgers stands at the free-throw line. He dribbles the basketball. He stops and shoots. The ball goes up in the air. Swish! Aaron nails it. He was just nine years old. But he made his first headline. He won a free-throw shooting contest. Aaron was on the front page of the local newspaper. Aaron was born in Chico, California, on December 2, 1983. He showed at an early age he was a good athlete.

Aaron shows it again in high school. He is the quarterback on the football team. He takes the snap. He runs from the **crowded** offensive line.

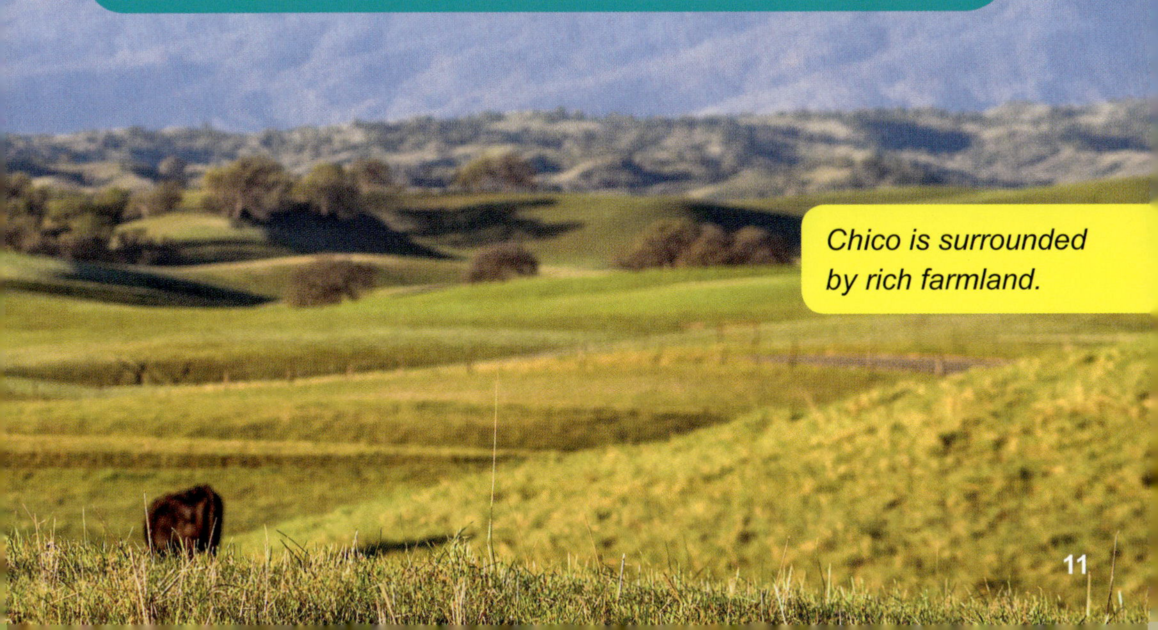

Chico is surrounded by rich farmland.

Aaron moves to his left. He keeps moving as he pulls his shoulder back. He fires the ball quickly. The receiver grabs the ball. He sneaks his feet into the end zone. It's a touchdown! Aaron was one of the best quarterbacks in school history.

But Aaron did not get the chance to go to a big college football team after high school. This was because he was shorter than most quarterbacks. He first played at Butte Community College.

Aaron proved himself at Butte. Then he got the chance to play for the University of California. Coach Jeff Tedford didn't worry about Aaron being short. Tedford trusted his talent.

FUN FACT

Aaron originally wanted to play for the University of Illinois.

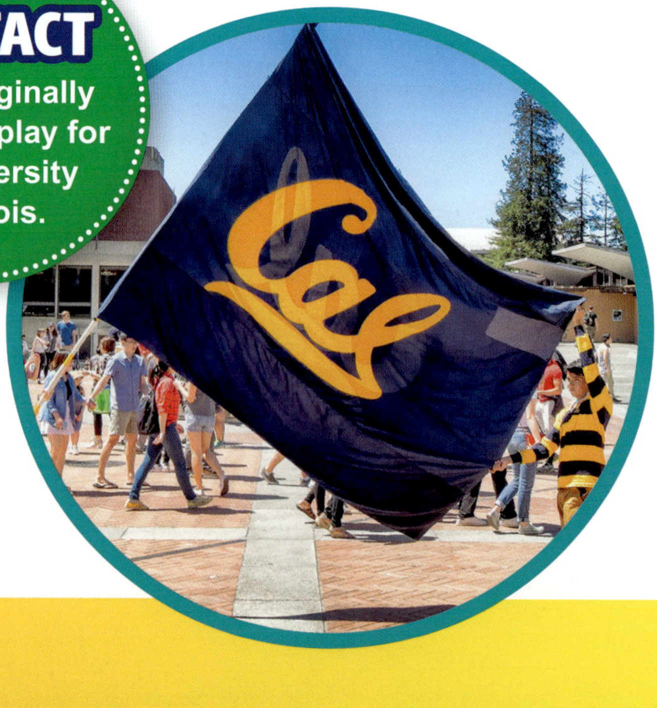

Aaron was a star quarterback for the Cal Golden Bears in 2003 and 2004.

Aaron stands tall in the middle of the **pocket**. He holds the ball near his blue Cal helmet. A running back cuts to the middle of the field. He is wide open. Aaron fires a pass. It's caught! The running back runs straight into the end zone. Aaron pumps his fist. Then he runs to his teammate who scored. They high-five. Aaron helped Cal win the 2003 Insight Bowl. He was named the game's Most Valuable Player (MVP).

Aaron played two years at Cal. Then he decided it was time to go pro. He entered the 2005 NFL Draft.

Aaron played his home games with Cal at California Memorial Stadium in Berkeley.

CAREER TIMELINE

1983

December 2, 1983
Rodgers is born in Chico, California.

2002

2002
Rodgers graduates from Pleasant Valley High School and heads to Butte Community College.

2003

2003
Rodgers transfers to the University of California where he plays for two seasons.

2005

April 23, 2005
Rodgers is drafted in the first round of the NFL Draft by the Packers.

2008

2008
Rodgers becomes Green Bay's starting quarterback.

2011

February 6, 2011
Rodgers leads Green Bay to a win in Super Bowl XLV.

2012

February 4, 2012
A season after winning the Super Bowl, Rodgers is named the NFL MVP.

2014

January 31, 2014
Rodgers wins his second NFL MVP award.

2017

January 22, 2017
Rodgers plays in his third career National Football Conference (NFC) Championship Game.

CHAPTER 3

A Busy Man

Aaron Rodgers grips the football. He looks to where he's about to throw it. He tosses the ball. It's caught! Everyone cheers. But this isn't an NFL game. This is Rodgers spending time with a child. This child has **cancer**. Rodgers spends a lot of time with kids fighting cancer. It's part of what he does away from football.

CAREER STATS

Through the 2018 season

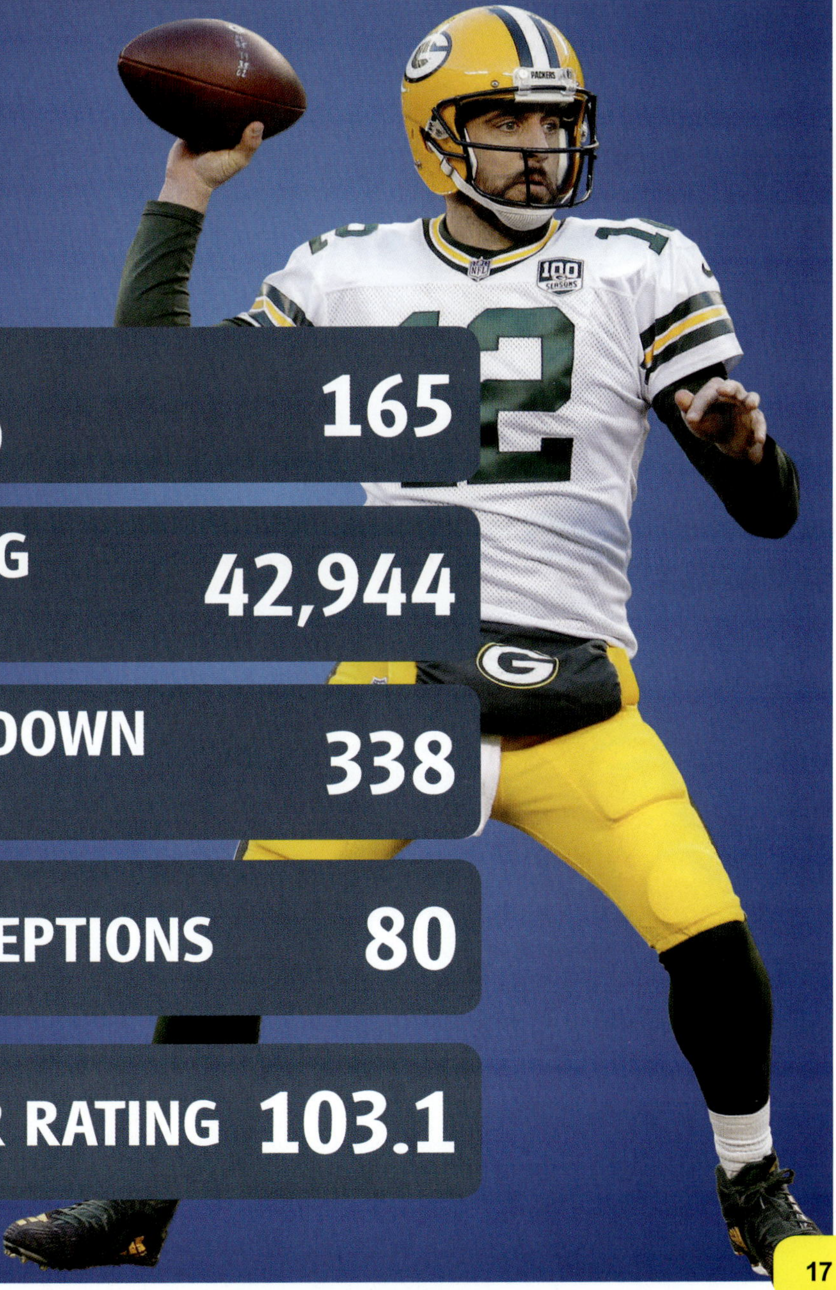

GAMES PLAYED	165
PASSING YARDS	42,944
TOUCHDOWN PASSES	338
INTERCEPTIONS	80
PASSER RATING	103.1

Rodgers and his girlfriend, retired race car driver Danica Patrick, attend a Milwaukee Bucks game in 2018.

Rodgers's work also takes him to Africa. Rodgers talks to a group of kids. He is working with a charity to provide hearing aids. Rodgers helps kids put the hearing aids in. Just like that, they can hear. Rodgers has spent time in other countries giving out hearing aids to those in need.

Packers fans can see Rodgers in different places in Wisconsin. Fans often see him at Milwaukee Bucks basketball games. Rodgers sits near the court with friends and family. He watches the games and cheers on the Bucks. Rodgers owns part of the team. He also cheers on other Wisconsin sports teams.

FUN FACT

Rodgers's brother Jordan played quarterback for Vanderbilt University.

Fans can also see Rodgers on TV. He pretends to do his championship belt celebration. But this time he is not celebrating a score. He is pretending to celebrate a good deal on car **insurance**. Rodgers appears in many commercials.

Rodgers signs autographs for fans at the 2012 NFL Pro Bowl.

CHAPTER 4

Top Quarterback

Aaron Rodgers sits in a nice blue suit. He is waiting patiently to hear his name. It is the 2005 NFL Draft. Rodgers thinks he could be one of the first players picked that year. But he is in for a surprise.

Twenty-one teams pass on Rodgers. Now, it is the Green Bay Packers' turn to pick. They call Rodgers's name. Relieved, he walks onto the stage. He smiles and holds up a green Packers jersey. Rodgers is now a member of the Packers.

FUN FACT

Rodgers thought he might be drafted by his hometown San Francisco 49ers, who had the No. 1 pick.

Rodgers holds up a Packers jersey after being drafted by Green Bay in 2005.

That fall, Rodgers stood on the sideline. He started his first NFL season as a **backup** to Brett Favre. Favre had been the Packers' star quarterback for years. Rodgers had to wait three seasons for a chance.

That chance came in 2008. Rodgers jogs onto the field that fall. Rodgers is now the starting quarterback. Soon, he will be on the field taking on the rival Minnesota Vikings. Some fans miss Favre. Rodgers has a lot to live up to.

FUN FACT

The Packers went 6–10 the first year Rodgers started. They did not have another losing record until 2017.

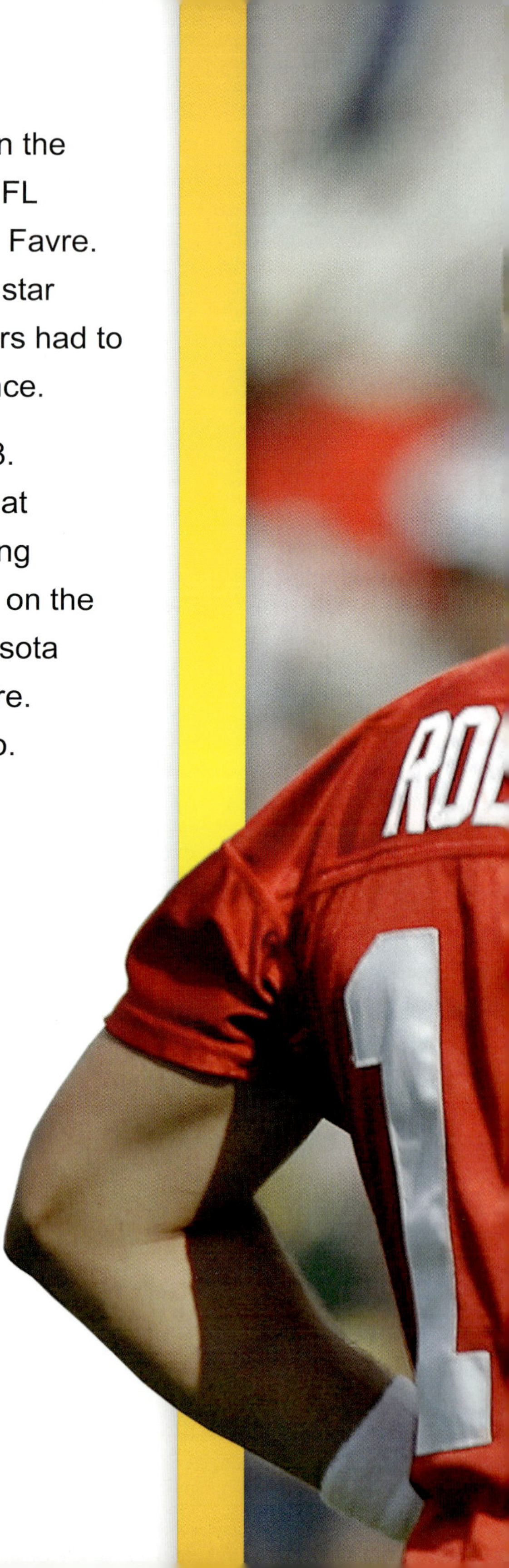

Rodgers learned under Brett Favre, one of the best quarterbacks in NFL history.

Rodgers salutes the fans as he walks off the field after a win over the Chicago Bears in 2018.

Rodgers stands with his knees bent. He calls for the ball. It's snapped back to him. Rodgers brings his arm back. It's a quick throw. It's caught! Fans were now seeing Rodgers's skills. He threw quick and accurate passes.

Packers fans knew what Rodgers could do. The world learned three years later. Rodgers played in the Super Bowl. After the Packers won, he held up the championship trophy. Packers fans hugged each other. They cheered loudly for Rodgers.

Rodgers held up two more trophies later on. In 2011, Rodgers was named the NFL MVP. He was **honored** again in 2014. Rodgers has become one of the best quarterbacks ever.

HAIL MARY

Rodgers takes the snap. He waits for the receivers to get to the end zone. He looks 60 yards down the field. Detroit Lions defenders close in. Rodgers gets away. He launches the ball. It soars in the air. Finally, it lands in the hands of a Packers receiver. Touchdown! Rodgers became known for making these risky passes. They are known as Hail Mary throws.

BEYOND THE BOOK

After reading the book, it's time to think about what you learned. Try the following exercises to jumpstart your ideas.

THINK

THAT'S NEWS TO ME. Aaron Rodgers became well-known for his Hail Mary passes. Learn more about that kind of play. Find an article online about a game where Aaron Rodgers threw one of these passes. Read more about what happened before that throw. What were other important moments in the game?

CREATE

SHARPEN YOUR RESEARCH SKILLS. Aaron Rodgers helped the Green Bay Packers to a Super Bowl. Where could you go to learn more about the history of the Packers? Create a research plan. Then, write a paragraph that says what your next step is.

SHARE

WHAT'S YOUR OPINION? In the book, it says that Aaron Rodgers is one of the best quarterbacks ever. Do you agree with this? Share your opinion with evidence to a classmate. Does the classmate find the argument convincing?

GROW

REAL-LIFE RESEARCH. What kind of place could you go to learn more about football and Aaron Rodgers? What are some other things you could learn by visiting this place?

RESEARCH NINJA

Visit www.ninjaresearcher.com/0356 to learn how to take your research skills and book report writing to the next level!

RESEARCH

DIGITAL LITERACY TOOLS

SEARCH LIKE A PRO
Learn about how to use search engines to find useful websites.

TEXT DETECTIVE
Explore how to zero in on the information you need most.

FACT OR FAKE?
Discover how you can tell a trusted website from an untrustworthy resource.

SHOW YOUR WORK
Research responsibly—learn how to cite sources.

WRITE

GET TO THE POINT
Learn how to express your main ideas.

PLAN OF ATTACK
Learn prewriting exercises and create an outline.

DOWNLOADABLE REPORT FORMS

Further Resources

BOOKS

Fishman, Jon M. *Football Superstar Aaron Rodgers*. Lerner Publications, 2019.

Myers, Dan. *Green Bay Packers*. Abdo Publishing, 2017.

Osborne, M.K. *Superstars of the Green Bay Packers*. Amicus, 2019.

WEBSITES

FACTSURFER

Factsurfer.com gives you a safe, fun way to find more information.

1. Go to www.factsurfer.com.
2. Enter "Aaron Rodgers" into the search box and click 🔍.
3. Select your book cover to see a list of related websites.

Glossary

backup: A backup is a player on the team that's there in case one of the main players cannot play. Aaron Rodgers was a backup to Brett Favre from 2005 to 2007.

cancer: Cancer is a serious disease that happens when bad cells destroy healthy organs and tissues. Rodgers spends his free time trying to bring joy to kids with cancer.

crowded: Something is crowded if there is not much room. Fans crowded into the stadium to watch Rodgers play quarterback.

grin: To grin means to have a large smile. Rodgers had a grin on his face after winning the Super Bowl.

honor: To honor means to give someone praise or an award. The NFL honored Rodgers twice as the league's most valuable player.

insurance: People pay for insurance so they can get paid if an accident or other loss happens. Rodgers has been in commercials for car insurance companies.

penalty: A penalty is a punishment for when a player does something that's not allowed. The defensive player got a penalty for hitting Rodgers after the play was over.

pocket: A team's offensive linemen protect the pocket where the quarterback stands before he throws. Rodgers stood in the pocket while looking for a receiver.

snap: The snap is when the quarterback receives the ball to start the play. Rodgers took the snap.

Index

PHOTO CREDITS

The images in this book are reproduced through the courtesy of: Jeff Haynes/Panini/AP Images, cover (center); Seth Wenig/AP Images, cover (right), pp. 3, 17 (Aaron Rodgers); Jeff Bukowski/Shutterstock Images, pp. 4, 15 (bottom), 16, 20; Eric Gay/AP Images, pp. 4–5; Red Line Editorial, pp. 6, 15 (timeline), 17 (chart); Marcio Jose Sanchez/AP Images, p. 7; Mark Humphrey/AP Images, p. 9; Paul Higley/Shutterstock Images, pp. 10–11; sevenMaps7/Shutterstock Images, pp. 11, 15 (top); cdrin/Shutterstock Images, p. 12; Paul Sakuma/AP Images, pp. 12–13; Aspen Photo/Shutterstock Images, p. 14; Morry Gash/AP Images, pp. 18–19, 24–25; Jim Mahoney/AP Images, p. 20–21; Scott Boehm/AP Images, p. 22; Julie Jacobson/AP Images, p. 23; Todd Rosenberg/AP Images, p. 26 (Aaron Rodgers); mark stephens photography/Shutterstock Images, p. 26 (sign); CE Photography/Shutterstock Images, p. 30.

ABOUT THE AUTHOR

Kevin Frederickson is a writer who lives with his goldendoodle in Cincinnati, Ohio. He has written other children's books throughout his decade-long career in the publishing industry.